Navigating Current and Emerging Army Recruiting Challenges

What Can Research Tell Us?

BETH J. ASCH

RAND ARROYO CENTER

Prepared for the United States Army
Approved for public release; distribution unlimited

For more information on this publication, visit www.rand.org/t/RR3107

Library of Congress Cataloging-in-Publication Data is available for this publication.

ISBN: 978-1-9774-0403-9

Cover: *SDI Productions/Getty Images*

Executive Summary

Recruiting is the foundation of the U.S. Army's ability to sustain its overall force levels, but recruiting has become very challenging. This report draws on a large body of research on military recruiting and examines tools and resources—including recruiters and recruiting management, selection and eligibility criteria, advertising, bonuses, and educational benefits—that could help the Army meet this challenge. It indicates that the Army could meet these challenges by taking advantages of recently developed tools to inform recruiting activities, explore opportunities to improve station productivity, exploit opportunities to better target the Army's outreach and recruiting resources in different market segments, consider adjustments to recruiter selection policy and redesign recruiter incentive plans to increase recruiter productivity, and coordinate recruiting and retention resource decisions.

This report is one in a series prepared specifically to synthesize several years of research about a common topic. The intent is to provide the Army's most senior leadership with an integrated view of recent years of Army-sponsored research, research that might not have achieved its full potential impact because it was presented to the Army as a series of independent research topics and findings. By looking across three to five years of research and identifying key unifying themes and recommendations, Army leadership can gain better visibility on some key issue areas and will have an additional source of information to inform key policy decisions and planning guidance. In this report, the research was sponsored by the Army as well as the Office of the Secretary of Defense and draws from more than 30 years of research.

This research was conducted within RAND Arroyo Center's Personnel, Training, and Health Program. RAND Arroyo Center, part of the RAND Corporation, is a federally funded research and development center (FFRDC) sponsored by the United States Army.

RAND operates under a "Federal-Wide Assurance" (FWA00003425) and complies with the *Code of Federal Regulations for the Protection of Human Subjects Under United States Law* (45 CFR 46), also known as "the Common Rule," as well as with the implementation guidance set forth in DoD Instruction 3216.02. As applicable, this compliance includes reviews and approvals by RAND's Institutional Review Board (the Human Subjects Protection Committee) and by the U.S. Army. The views of sources used in this report are solely their own and do not represent the official policy or position of U.S. Department of Defense or the U.S. government.

(This page is intentionally left blank.)

Contents

(This page is intentionally left blank.)

Figures

(This page is intentionally left blank.)

Tables

(This page is intentionally left blank.)

Summary

The U.S. Army is facing a period of intense recruiting challenges—a confluence of internal and external factors shaping the recruiting environment. On the one hand, the Army recruiting mission is growing as the service is set to increase the size of the force. On the other hand, potential recruits have excellent civilian employment opportunities, as the current unemployment rate, as of this writing, is at a near-historic low (U.S. Department of Labor, 2019). Together, these conditions mean that the Army will have to work harder to entice recruits to join. But the Army will also have to work smarter, given limited available resources to support its recruiting effort.

In practical terms, the Army must take a hard look at its entire recruiting enterprise and find ways to make it more productive and less costly. Drawing on a large body of research on military recruiting, this report examines tools and resources that could help the Army meet this challenge—including in such areas as recruiters and recruiter management, selection and eligibility criteria for new recruits advertising expenditures and allocation, enlistment bonuses, and educational benefits. Among the many research and policy options available, the following opportunities offer the most promise in the near term.

1. *Take advantage of recently developed tools to inform recruiting activities.* There is no one-size-fits-all solution to developing the most-effective recruiting program or selection criteria. The most-effective policies will depend on prevailing circumstances, including budget levels, missions, economic conditions, program implementation, Army objectives, and the planning horizon. Tools such as the Recruiting Resource Model, the Recruit Selection Tool, and the Recruiting Difficulty Index, discussed in this report, can help the Army navigate this complex decision process. These tools can be used to identify an efficient level and mix of recruiting resources under a variety of environmental conditions, optimize recruit selection criteria, and predict near-term recruiting difficulties.

2. *Explore opportunities to improve station productivity by setting station missions to better reflect differences in recruiting markets and the resulting difficulties that recruiters face.* Station success or failure is substantially affected by station performance goals, but mission difficulty varies considerably across stations because of differences in market demographics, economic conditions, market size, and other factors. Recruiter productivity responds to performance goals, but the degree of that response varies with the level of mission difficulty.

3. *Exploit opportunities to better target the Army's outreach and recruiting resources in different market segments,* including different geographic areas, older recruits, college-market recruits, and other demographics. For example, the Army might focus outreach efforts in New England on career aspirations of potential recruits, while those in the South might focus on intangible benefits of Army service, such as patriotism. The Recruiting Resource Model and other tools could be refined to assess the optimal allocation and cost-effectiveness of such targeted policies. Related to outreach, the Army

needs a better understanding of the effects of its social media presence and the internet on recruiting.

4. *Consider adjustments to recruiter selection policy to increase recruiting productivity.* Research demonstrates that individual recruiter characteristics—such as gender, race, education, scores on the Armed Forces Qualification Test, military experience, career management field, and age—can be linked with significant increases in recruiter productivity. Moreover, recruiters assigned to their home state are more effective. That said, there are differences in recruiter productivity that cannot be attributed to observed characteristics, suggesting that also using personality screens that incorporate "soft" factors could improve recruiter selection.

5. *Redesign recruiter incentive plans to include both individual and team-based incentives to increase recruiter productivity and resource effectiveness.* Team-based incentives can encourage cooperation within a station, but individual recruiter incentives should also be carefully managed because these incentives affect individual recruiter productivity. Recruiter incentives could be as cost-effective or more cost-effective than monetary incentives targeted toward recruits. Recruiting resources such as recruiters, advertising, and bonuses are effective in expanding enlistments, but their effectiveness is affected by recruiter effort and recruiter incentives to reach out and process more enlistments.

6. *Coordinate recruiting and retention resource decisions.* The most cost-effective strategy for meeting end strength goals could be to retain rather than recruit more soldiers—particularly in career fields where training costs are high. Thus, recruiting and retention policies and resource decisions should be synchronized.

The tools and opportunities identified here focus on addressing the Army's short-term recruiting challenges. In the longer run, the Army, together with the other services, should consider ways to help bridge the military-civilian divide. The youth population often has an incorrect or narrow understanding of what military service entails, how it affects career potential, and its effects on family and personal relationships—all of which can lead to more recruiter effort and resources to induce individuals to join the military. The Army needs to get out ahead of these trends and develop a cost-effective strategy that is informed by metrics, data, and analysis to bridge the divide.

Acknowledgments

The author would like to thank Michael Linick, director of RAND Arroyo Center's Personnel, Training, and Health program, as well as Shanthi Nataraj, who was the associate director of the program at the time this research was conducted. This report benefited from the help of LTC William (Hank) Waggy, who provided contextual background information, and RAND colleagues David Knapp and Barbara Bicksler, who provided comments on an earlier draft. Their help is very much appreciated. I would also like to thank two reviewers of an earlier draft, Jennie Wenger at RAND, and Curtis Simon, professor of economics at Clemson University. Their input benefited the report substantially.

(This page is intentionally left blank.)

Navigating Current and Emerging Army Recruiting Challenges: What Can Research Tell Us?

Introduction

Recruiting is the foundation of the all-volunteer force in the United States. Meeting accession requirements is critical to sustaining overall force levels, given a relatively stable experience mix in the enlisted force and the general lack of lateral entry into the active force. Furthermore, the average quality of the enlisted force overall from grades E-1 to E-9 is largely determined by the quality of those who are recruited in the junior grades (Asch, Romley, and Totten, 2005; Asch and Warner, 1996).

Yet recruiting is also very challenging. Less than 30 percent of young adults are estimated to meet enlistment eligibility criteria, and even among those who meet minimum criteria, the Army aims for high-quality entrants who have better civilian employment opportunities and prospects for college attendance (Lewin Group, 2013). A high-quality recruit is one who scores in the top half of the Armed Forces Qualification Test (AFQT) score distribution and is a high school graduate, typically described as one with a Tier 1 credential.[1]

In addition, fewer than one in ten young adults expresses a positive propensity to enlist (Joint Advertising and Marketing Research Studies [JAMRS], 2018), meaning that less than 10 percent of 16- to 21-year-olds respond with "definitely" or "probably" when asked how likely is it that they would be serving on active duty in the U.S. Army in the next two years.[2] An implication of youth propensity today, or lack thereof, is that the majority of enlistees—two-thirds of them—are from the negatively propensed group.[3] Consequently, a large part of the military recruiting effort involves converting youth who are negatively propensed to join the military into actual enlistments. Not surprisingly, then, recruiting is also costly. Army recruiting costs were $1.5 billion annually on average between 2001 and 2014 in 2016 dollars (Knapp et al., 2018).

---

[1] The AFQT is a composite of the scores received by the applicant on the tests for arithmetic reasoning, mathematical knowledge, word knowledge, and paragraph comprehension. The AFQT score is expressed on a percentile scale that reflects the applicants standing relative to the national population of men and women ages 18–23. Tier 1 refers to high school graduates and nongraduates with at least 15 hours of college credit (Office of the Under Secretary of Defense for Personnel and Readiness, 1997–2016).

[2] The percentage of young people expressing a positive propensity varies across service and overtime within a service, but it is still at most around 10 percent for any given service in recent years.

[3] Using youth poll data from 2001 to 2003 and youth attitudinal tracking survey data from 1995 to 1999, Joint Advertising and Marketing Research Studies estimated that 38.8 percent of youth who are positively propensed actually enlist, and 6.7 percent of the negatively propensed group enlists (Ford et al., 2009). Given that an average of 8 percent of respondents state a positive propensity to enlist (and 92 percent state a negative propensity), the implication is that 66.5 percent of enlistments come from the negatively propensed group.

The Army has several tools at its disposal to assist in meeting its recruiting goals, including advertising, enlistment bonuses, the recruiter force, and recruit selection standards, as well as other policies that the Army does not have discretion over but could possibly influence, such as overall military pay levels, benefit levels, and annual raises. A considerable body of research has been conducted since even before the advent of the all-volunteer force in 1973 on the effectiveness and cost of these policy tools, the factors affecting individual decisions to enlist and overall enlistment supply, and resource management—especially the management of recruiters.

This report presents a summary of the available research findings on Army recruiting that could help Army leadership navigate current and emerging recruiting challenges.[4] It summarizes research findings related to the enlistment decision and estimated enlistment supply and resource effectiveness, highlights new resource management tools that have been developed to help leadership with resource decisionmaking, and discusses emerging recruiting challenges and areas where the Army requires more information to successfully meet these challenges. The report begins with contextual information on recruiting and recent recruiting trends.

Recent Historical Context

The Army's recruiting goal is substantially larger than that of the other services, about double since the early 2000s (Figure 1), which magnifies its recruiting challenges. The magnitude of the goal depends on the desired end strength and on separations of those already serving. The Army accession goal hovered around 75,000 to 80,000 recruits until 2008, declined to 57,000 by 2014, and has been increasing since then.

Operations in Iraq and Afghanistan beginning in 2002 stressed the Army, including its ability to meet its recruiting mission. The Army failed to meet its recruiting goal in 2005, and past studies found that these operations had a negative effect on recruiting, although the estimated effect varies (Asch et al., 2010; Christensen, 2017; Simon and Warner, 2009). Recruit quality, as measured by educational credentials or the percentage of Army accessions that were Tier 1, also fell in the middle of the decade (Figure 2, left panel). Tier 1 recruits are deemed better quality because they are less likely to attrite during the first enlistment term (Buddin, 2005). (Aptitude test scores, discussed later, are additional metric of recruit quality.) Another indicator of recruiting difficulty during this period is the percentage of recruits who have prior service, which increased, especially in 2007 (Figure 2, right panel). The Army limits prior service enlistments but relaxes those limits during difficult recruiting conditions. Knapp et al. (2018) report that the Army also began increasing the fraction of recruits receiving medical and conduct enlistment waivers in fiscal year (FY) 2005.

---

[4] This paper focuses on Regular Army recruiting. Research on Reserve Component recruiting for the Army Reserve and the Army National Guard is far less extensive.

Figure 1. Enlisted Accession Goals by Service

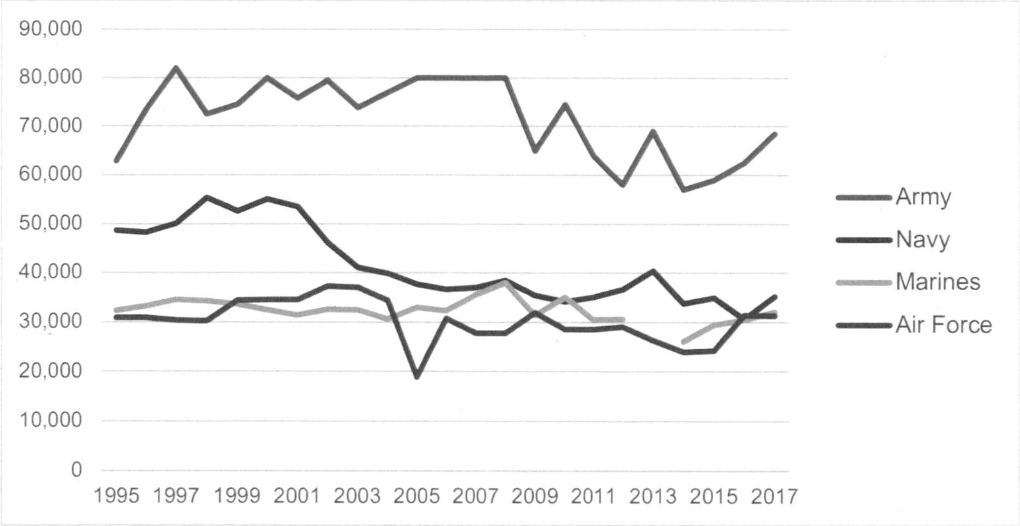

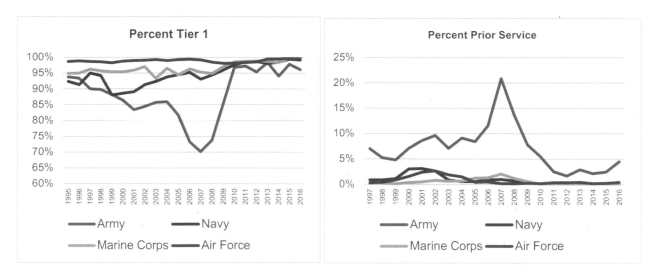

SOURCE: Office of the Under Secretary of Defense for Personnel and Readiness, 1997–2016.
NOTE: Marine Corps data for 2013 are missing.

Figure 2. Enlisted Accessions That Are Tier 1 (Left) and Prior Service (Right), by Service

SOURCE: Office of the Under Secretary of Defense for Personnel and Readiness, 1997–2016.

To respond to the stresses on recruiting that began in 2002, the Army not only expanded recruit eligibility but also expanded recruiting resources including average quick-ship and enlistment bonuses levels,[5] number of recruiters, and advertising expenditures (Knapp et al., 2018). Military pay relative to civilian pay also increased (Figure 3). The increases in military

---

[5] *Quick-ship* bonuses are paid for recruits who ship to training within 60 days of enlistment. Shipping within 30 days yields a higher bonus than shipping within 31–60 days. Enlistment bonuses are available to those who enlist in specific Army jobs.

pay started, rather fortuitously, even before operations began in Iraq and Afghanistan; the National Defense Authorization Act of 2000 required basic pay increases that were greater than the Employment Cost Index from 2000 through 2006, and it decreased the expected out-of-pocket costs for housing from 20 percent in 2000 to zero in 2005. Although military pay was increasing, civilian pay trended downward from 1999 to 2012 (Hosek et al., 2018), thereby improving relative military pay. Improvements in relative military pay are important because past research shows that the number of Army high-quality recruits increases when relative military pay increases (Asch et al., 2010).[6] Despite the expansion of recruit eligibility standards and increase in relative military pay, the Army's cost per accession increased from $15,500 in 2004 to $27,700 in 2009 (Knapp et al., 2018).

After 2009, recruiting conditions improved. The economy stalled as a result of the Great Recession that began in fall 2008, thereby improving the attractiveness of Army service relative to recruits' opportunities in the civilian workplace. Research shows an increase in high-quality enlistments when the unemployment rate rises (Asch et al., 2010; Knapp et al., 2018). The strong relationship between the strength of the economy and high-quality recruits is shown in Figure 4.[7] In addition, the number of Army deployments fell markedly after 2010, and the Army accession mission began to decline as did the overall enlisted force size. Military pay, as measured by regular military compensation (RMC), was also relatively constant from 2010 to 2016 (Hosek et al., 2018).

---

[6] Table 1.1 summarizes estimates from recent studies.

[7] Note that Figure 1.4 does not adjust for other factors that might have changed over time (e.g., it does not hold other factors, such as recruiting resources, accession requirements, or deployment frequency and length, equal). Unemployment rates over time for age subgroups also follow a similar pattern as for the overall adult unemployment rate, although the unemployment rate for young adults ages 16–24 is uniformly higher (Statista, 2019).

Figure 3. Enlisted Military Pay Relative to Median Civilian Pay for Male and Female High School Graduates, Ages 18–22

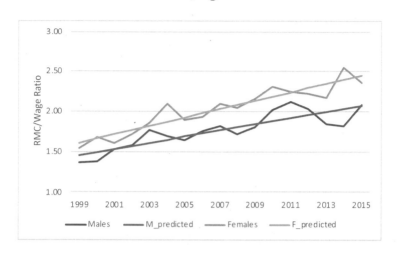

SOURCE: Hosek et al., 2018.
NOTE: Military pay is measured as RMC for an E-4 with four years of service. The ratio is for RMC relative to the median civilian pay for 18- to 22-year old workers with high school (and without additional education) who had more than 35 hours of work in the year and more than 35 usual weekly hours of work. *M_predicted* refers to the trend line for males, and *F_predicted* refers to the trend lind for females.

Figure 4. High-Quality Army Enlisted Accessions and Adult Unemployment Rate

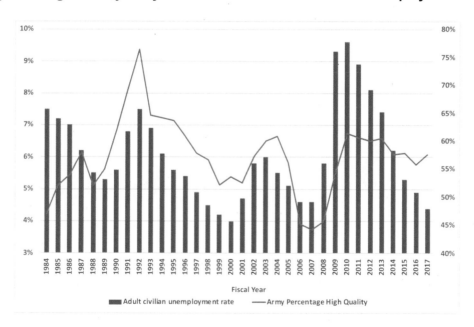

The Navy, Air Force, and Marine Corps responded to the improved recruiting conditions in 2009 by increasing recruit quality and specifically the percentage of recruits who are scored as AFQT Categories I–IIIA (Figure 5), sustaining percentages that exceeded 70 percent Categories I–IIIA through 2016. U.S. Department of Defense (DoD) guidelines are that 60 percent of recruits are AFQT Categories I–IIIA and 90 percent are Tier 1. The other services well exceeded the DoD guideline after 2009.

In contrast, the Army responded to the improved recruiting conditions by cutting resources and chose to reduce the percentage of recruits in AFQT Categories I–IIIA down to the 60 percent DoD guideline. Knapp et al. (2018) show that the percentage of Army recruits receiving bonuses, average bonus amounts, and Army advertising expenditures dropped dramatically in 2009. Furthermore, Army-enlisted recruits with prior military service (Figure 2, right) and those receiving medical or conduct waivers dropped considerably in 2009 compared with 2008. The Army also increased Tier 1 recruits dramatically in 2009 (Figure 2, left) and kept the percentage Tier 1 at or above 90 percent thereafter. Even with fewer recruiting resources, the Army met its overall accession mission between 2009 and 2017 and even substantially exceeded it in 2010 and 2012.

Figure 5. AFQT Categories I–IIIA Enlisted Accessions by Service

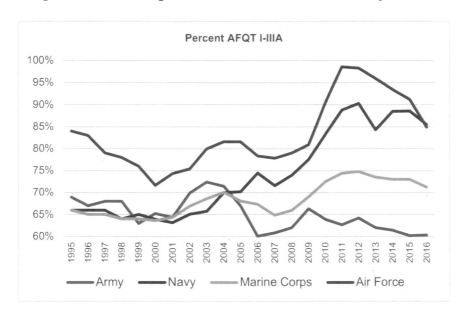

SOURCE: Office of the Under Secretary of Defense for Personnel and Readiness, 1997–2016.
NOTE: A *high-quality accession* is defined as Tier I recruits in AFQT Categories I–IIIA.

The Army's differing strategy when recruiting conditions improved suggested that the Army focused on reducing recruiting costs while achieving its overall recruiting mission and meeting DoD benchmarks of 90 percent Tier 1 and 60 percent AFQT Categories I–IIIA recruits. The other services focused on achieving their overall mission while increasing recruit quality above the benchmarks. The different strategies raise the question of what level of recruit quality is appropriate: Are the DoD benchmarks still relevant, should recruit quality increase, or should recruiting costs decrease when recruiting conditions improve? Put differently, how should the services, and the Army specifically, reap the benefits of a less-challenging recruiting market? The Army's approach would be more appropriate than the other services if the DoD benchmarks are still relevant. On the other hand, if higher recruit quality is required, increasing the higher recruit quality produced by the other services would be more appropriate, although as discussed in more detail in the following section, research shows that increasing resources other than military pay might be a more cost-effective means of increasing recruit quality.

Recruiting has become more challenging in recent years, however. The Army's total recruiting mission has increased from 57,000 in 2014 to 76,500 in 2018. Furthermore, the economy has dramatically improved. The adult unemployment rate reached a high of 9.6 percent in 2010, but, by 2014, had fallen to 7.4 percent, as shown in Figure 4. In June 2019, adult unemployment was 3.7 percent. As mentioned earlier, research shows that Army high-quality recruits fall, given no other changes, when the economy improves. Tools developed at the RAND Corporation (discussed in the following section), such as the Recruiting Resource Model (RRM), can help the Army assess the relative efficiency of different resource mixes when conditions such as the strength of the economy are changing.

Understanding the Decision to Enlist

Fundamental to successful recruiting is understanding the factors affecting the decision of young people, especially high-quality young people, to enlist. These decisions are typically modeled within an occupational choice framework, where individuals are assumed to enlist if the expected value of joining the military exceeds the opportunity cost of not doing so. The decision involves comparing the compensation and nonmonetary benefits available in the military with what is expected in the civilian sector. The opportunity cost is the expected value of alternative civilian pursuits, such as civilian employment or pursuing additional education.

Army service is relatively arduous and involves the exposure to risk and potential loss of life, but it also offers many nonmonetary benefits, including patriotism and pride in service to country, the opportunity to travel, acquiring training and generally having access to stable employment. Military service can also be a stepping stone to better future civilian opportunities, if skills acquired in the military are highly transferable to civilian employment. Research supports this, showing that greater college aspirations among recent high school graduates is associated with a higher likelihood of joining the military compared with directly entering the civilian labor market (Kleykamp, 2006). Put differently, attending college and military service could be complementary career aspirations with military service operating as a pathway toward college enrollment. Military service also provides monetary benefits, including basic pay and allowances and, if qualified, special and incentive pays, bonuses, and ultimately retirement pay.

The importance of pay, patriotism, and meaningful work is revealed in DoD surveys of young adults and new recruits. The top factors reported as the number one considerations in selecting a job in the spring 2016 DoD Youth Poll were having a higher-than-average income, maintaining a good work-life balance, and finding meaningful work (JAMRS, 2017b). In the March 2018 New Recruit Survey, the top five reasons Army recruits wanted to join the Army were pride or self-esteem/honor (67 percent), travel (66 percent), life betterment (64 percent), gain experience or work skills (59 percent), and pay or money (56 percent). The majority of new

Army recruits (62 percent) in the 2018 survey also indicated that they view the Army as a stepping stone for their future career outside the Army.

Analyses of young people's decisions to enlist instead of work or attend college also show that employment considerations affect the enlistment decision. Young people who reported working more hours in their current job, having low wages, or were not employed were more likely to enlist when other factors were held constant (Kilburn and Klerman, 1999). However, variables related to the expected return to college, specifically their AFQT score, increased the likelihood of attending college rather than enlisting, suggesting that the targeting of recruiting to those who have higher expected returns to college will not be as successful as targeting those with lower returns.

A concern at the beginning of the all-volunteer force and one that has occasionally emerged in recent years is whether those who enlist are drawn from the poorest segments of society. Analyses of individuals' enlistment decisions consistently show that those with lower socioeconomic status are more likely to enlist (Kilburn and Klerman, 1999; Kleykamp, 2006). In particular, Kilburn and Klerman (1999) find that the likelihood of enlistment is greater among high school seniors and graduates with lower family incomes, more siblings (so more sharing of family resources), and less-educated mothers, other characteristics held constant.

That said, research suggests that accessions come from all income levels, although studies find that they disproportionately come from households in the middle of the income distribution and not from those in the lowest or highest percentiles of household income (Kane, 2005; Lien, Lawler, and Shuford, 2012; Watkins and Sherk, 2008). Figure 6 replicates the findings from Lien, Lawler, and Shuford (2012), which linked DoD non–prior service accessions to the median income of recruits' home-of-record census tract, thereby allowing the researchers to classify accessions by the income quintiles of the census tract from where the accessions were from. Figure 6 shows the percentage of accessions that come from each quintile of the distribution of census tract household income (blue bars). If accessions were evenly distributed across census tract household income levels, the percentage would be 20 percent for each quintile in Figure 6. Instead, 17.8 percent and 18.5 percent of accessions come from the bottom and top quintiles, respectively. Furthermore, Figure 6 compares non-prior service accessions with the 18- to 24-year-old population (purple bars). Note that the population of 17-to-24-year-olds is also not evenly distributed across census tract household incomes levels. The broader population is more likely to be concentrated in the lowest quintile. Comparing the distributions, accessions are more likely to come from the middle- and high-income segments relative to the population, although, unlike the Kilburn and Klerman (1999) analysis, this comparison does not hold characteristics other than income constant, including family size.

Figure 6. FY 2011 DoD Non–Prior Service Accessions Compared with Youth (18–24 Year Olds) Population, by Household Census Tract Income Quintile

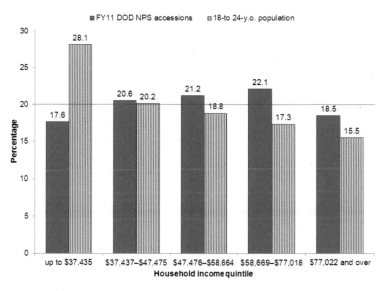

a. Source: CNA tabulations of DMDC FY11 DOD NPS accession data and 2006–2010 ACS data, adjusted to 2011 dollars.

SOURCE: Lien, Lawler, and Shuford, 2012. This figure reproduces Figure 5 in the Lien, Lawler and Shuford report.

Accessions also are not evenly distributed across geographic areas. Studies consistently find evidence of the Southern military tradition. Since the beginning of the all-volunteer force, accessions are predominately from Southern states. For example, in 2010, Florida, South Carolina, and Georgia had the highest ratio of accessions to the 18–24-year-old population, and Lien, Lawler, and Shuford (2012) find that, relative to the population, accessions were overrepresented in the South (at 1.21) and evenly represented in the West (at 1.0). The North Central region and Northeast were underrepresented (0.92 and 0.70, respectively). Relative to the population, recruits are also more educated and are overrepresented among rural areas and underrepresented among urban areas (Kane, 2005). The better education of recruits likely reflects the military's eligibility criteria and preference for high school graduates, while the overrepresentation from rural areas could reflect thinner job market opportunities in those areas.

These geographic differences raise the question of whether there are also political differences among accessions and whether recruiting is more difficult in blue or Democratic-leaning states. Survey results indicate that confidence in military leadership differs by political party. In 2012, 42 percent of Democrats in the General Social Survey reported a great deal of confidence in the military, compared with 68 percent of Republicans (Liebert and Golby, 2017). Wenger and McHugh (2008) examine this issue using county-level voting data and data on Marine Corps enlistments. They found county differences in enlistments—some counties produced more Marine Corps recruits, even after controlling for differences in population and economic opportunities, but voting behavior explained very little of this difference. In fact, the study actually found that red or Republican-leaning counties produced fewer Marine accessions than similar blue counties. The findings suggest that the red state–blue state divide is overly simplistic and overlooks differences within states and counties on factors affecting the enlistment decision.

One of those factors is having a family member who has served in the military. Individuals do not make their enlistment decision in a vacuum, and their decisions could be shaped by the advice of family, friends, and societal attitudes toward military service. Individuals living in an area with a high concentration of military employment are more likely to enlist (Kleykamp, 2006). Furthermore, studies find that individuals are more likely to enlist if they have a family member who has served or is serving (Kilburn and Klerman, 1999; Kleykamp, 2006).

The majority (63 percent) of new recruits in the 2016 New Recruit Survey reported having an immediate family member who is serving or has served, with 27 percent stating they had a parent who has served. These percentages are higher than the youth population in general. Although 53 percent of young people ages 16–24 in the United States report in a 2016 survey that they have an immediate family member (e.g., parent, sibling, grandparent) who has served in the military, only 15 percent of youth reported having a parent who has served (JAMRS, 2017a).

As discussed by Rostker, Klerman, and Cotugno (2014), the military has become a "family business," but the percentage of youth with a family connection to the military has been declining over time. This is attributable in part to smaller military strength over time and in part to the passing of the World War II generation. Survey results from Pew Research Center (2011) found that while 77 percent of adults ages 50 and older say they have an immediate family member who had served in the military, only one-third of those ages 18 to 29 said so.

Estimating Enlistment Supply and Resource Effectiveness

The enlistment decision can also be shaped by the military's recruiting establishment and how it sets recruiting resources, as well as how Congress sets military compensation. In the case of the Army, this includes the selection, training, and allocation of recruiters throughout the country; how recruiters are managed in terms of how their missions are assigned and the incentives available to reward recruiter productivity; the level of advertising expenditures and allocation across media type; enlistment bonus budgets; the selection and eligibility criteria for new recruits; and the availability of waivers.

Studies that examine recruiting resource effectiveness typically focus on enlistments in aggregate at a point in time in a given geographic area, building on models of the individual enlistment decision. They estimate how changes in the number of high-quality enlistments in a given geographic area—such as a state, Military Entrance Processing Station, or Army company—at a point in time are related to such variables as military pay, bonuses, civilian pay, the civilian unemployment rate, deployment length and frequency, demographic and job characteristics and variables that capture the services' recruiting effort (such as numbers of recruiters), the numerical quotas they face, and advertising.

A large number of studies have been conducted since the beginning of the all-volunteer force in 1973 and have used varied methods and data to estimate the effects of these variables. While estimates differ across studies, they consistently find that high-quality enlistments increase when military pay increases relative to civilian pay; when the civilian economy deteriorates as measured by the unemployment rate; and when advertising, enlistment bonuses, and recruiters increase. Tables 1–3 summarize the estimates from recent studies using Army data.

Military Pay and the Unemployment Rate

Studies estimate a pay elasticity of between 0.70 to 1.15 for the Army (Table 1). *Elasticity* is defined as the percentage change in high-quality enlistments associated with a 1-percent change in a given variable—in this case, military pay relative to civilian pay. Using FYs 2000–2008 data, Asch et al. (2010) estimated an elasticity of high-quality contracts with respect to relative military pay of 1.15. This implies that if the level of military pay was to rise by 10 percent relative to civilian wage opportunities, enlistment of high-quality youth would rise by 11.5 percent.

Consistent with the trends shown in Figure 5, it is unsurprising that studies consistently find a relationship between high-quality contracts and the civilian unemployment rate, all else being equal (Table 1). For example, Knapp et al. (2018) estimate an elasticity of high-quality contracts with respect to the unemployment rate to be about 0.3 using Army data from 2012 to 2015, implying that halving the civilian unemployment rate (e.g., from 10 to 5 percent) would reduce high-quality enlistment by 15 percent, all else equal. On a base of 50,000 high-quality enlistments annually in the Army, that would mean about 7,500 fewer individuals would need to be recruited. The range of estimates in the table reflects different time periods, analytic approaches, and unit of analysis.

Table 1. Estimated Elasticities of High-Quality Contracts with Respect to Relative Pay and Unemployment Rate

Study	Service	Data Type and Time Period	Relative Pay	Unemployment
Knapp et al., 2018	Army	Monthly by company, 2012–2015	N/A	0.30
Asch et al., 2010	Army	Quarterly by state, 2000–2008	1.15	0.11
Simon and Warner, 2007	Army	Quarterly by state, 1996–2005	0.70	0.42
Warner and Simon, 2004	Army	Quarterly by state, 1989–2003	0.71–0.81	0.25–0.31
Simon and Warner, 2003	Army	Monthly by state, 1989–1997	0.78	0.22
Warner, Simon, and Payne, 2001 (mean[a])	Various	Various, pre-drawdown	0.75	0.62

SOURCE: Adapted from Warner, 2010.
[a] From Appendix B of Warner, Simon, and Payne, 2001.

Advertising and Bonuses

Studies of Army advertising show that recruiting effects vary with media type and scale of advertising. Threshold and saturation points imply an S-shaped relationship between high-quality contracts and advertising. Low levels of advertising yield few impressions and have little effect; higher expenditures—and more impressions—are needed to have an effect, but eventually the market is saturated with the advertising, and, at high levels of expenditure, additional advertising again has little effect. Dertouzos and Garber (2003) used data from the mid-1980s and from 1993 to 1997 and found that the inflection points of the S-curves differ across media types that they considered. Only for large budgets was national television advertising cost-effective because larger expenditures are needed for television advertising to reach an audience. Knapp et al. (2018) found broadly similar S-curve results for television advertising using more recent Army data from 2012 to 2015, although the study found that television advertising was less effective at lower expenditure levels than the Dertouzos and Garber study.

That said, advertising is only as effective as the content for the target audience and the media used. Researchers have not assessed content effectiveness in terms of its effect on expanding the number of high-quality enlistments. Furthermore, the effectiveness of content could vary across different domains. For example, advertising about pride and service to country could resonate more in some parts of the country than others, while advertising about career benefits and educational benefits might be more effective elsewhere. Finally, traditional media such as radio and magazines are being replaced by social media and the internet, and less is known about the recruiting effectiveness of social media outreach. These points are discussed further in the next sections.

The services also make use of enlistment bonuses as an incentive to expand enlistment supply and channel recruits into hard-to-fill skill areas or for longer enlistment terms. Depending on model specification, estimates of the elasticity of high-quality enlistment with respect to expected bonus amount vary from 0.04 to 0.17 (Table 2). These estimates imply that a doubling of the average enlistment bonus (a 100-percent increase) would expand high-quality enlistments by between 4 to 17 percent. Thus, the market-expansion effect of bonuses is relatively modest.

Table 2. Estimated Elasticities of High-Quality Contracts with Respect to Enlistment Bonuses

Study	Service	Data Type and Time Period	Enlistment Bonus
Knapp et al., 2018	Army	Monthly by company, 2012–2015	0.04–0.13[a]
Asch et al., 2010	Army	Quarterly by state, 2000–2008	0.06–0.17
Simon and Warner, 2003	Army	Monthly by state, 1989–1997	0.12
Literature review mean[b]	Various	Various, pre-drawdown	0.06

SOURCE: Adapted from Warner, 2010.
[a] Estimate varies with level of average bonus level and percent eligibility.
[b] From Appendix B of Warner, Simon, and Payne, 2001.

Enlistment bonuses, however, could have other effects. A unique controlled experiment in the mid-1980s found larger bonus effects on enlistees' skill and term of enlistment choices than on market expansion (Polich, Dertouzos, and Press, 1986). The estimated market expansion effect on high-quality contracts was consistent with later studies, implying an enlistment bonus elasticity of about 0.07 to 0.08. But in the skill areas targeted by the bonuses, high-quality enlistments rose sharply, between 32 and 42 percent. Furthermore, the bonuses significantly increased the number of individuals willing to make a longer-term commitment to the military. Evidence from the Air Force, using more-recent data, also shows that offering larger bonuses induced longer enlistment term choices. Simon and Warner (2009) found that $5,000 spread between four- and six-year enlistment bonuses increased six-year contracts in the Air Force by 30 percentage points.

Another advantage of bonuses is that they can be deployed immediately. Funds can be reprogrammed within a fiscal year, and bonuses can be directed to recruits almost immediately. In contrast, advertising programs have to be designed and planned, and television spots often have to be purchased upfront and in advance. Similarly, recruiters need to be assigned and trained, and it takes time for them to reach full productivity.

Educational Benefits

Educational benefits are another incentive for high-quality enlistment. The Army used educational incentives intensively in the 1980s and 1990s by adding Army College Fund "kickers"—an additional educational benefit on top of the benefits available to all recruits who participated in the G.I. Bill program (known as the Montgomery GI Bill). The Navy introduced its own Navy College Fund program in 1990. These kickers gave the Army (and Navy) a leg up on the other services by providing an incentive that was not available elsewhere.

Estimates by Simon and Warner (2003) indicate that elimination of these kicker programs would have reduced Army high-quality enlistment by about 6 percent and Navy high-quality enlistment by about 4 percent. That is, about one-third of Army College Fund enlistments would not have enlisted in the absence of the program, and about 20 percent of Navy College Fund recipients would not have. Simon and Warner (2003) concluded that educational benefits are a reasonably cost-effective recruiting tool compared with other recruiting resources.

In August 2009, Congress created the Post-9/11 GI Bill program, dramatically increasing educational benefits for all military recruits to roughly double the real educational benefits compared with the Montgomery GI Bill program (Simon, Negrusa, and Warner, 2010). Because the Army eliminated the Army College Fund (and the Navy eliminated the Navy College Fund), there was no longer a differential educational enlistment incentive for active Army and Navy recruits. In a study of the recruiting and retention effects of the Post-9/11 GI Bill program, Wenger et al. (2017) found that the program had little, if any, effect on high-quality recruiting. Focus groups suggested that new recruits were aware of the program but lacked detailed knowledge of the benefit. The study also found that the program reduced continuation, but this effect was somewhat mitigated by the provision that qualified members could transfer benefits to dependents.

Recruiters and Recruiter Management

Recruiters contact and process applicants, and research shows that high-quality enlistments increase with the size of the recruiter force; studies typically estimate a recruiter elasticity of about 0.5, implying that high-quality enlistments increase by about 5 percent when the stock of Army recruiters increases by 10 percent (see Table 3). However, the positive relationship between recruiters and enlistments is not automatic. Recruiters make up a workforce, and they are a human resource that must be properly managed to be effective and efficient.

Table 3. Estimated Elasticities of High-Quality Contracts with Respect to Recruiters

Study	Service	Data Type and Time Period	Recruiters
Knapp et al., 2018	Army	Monthly by company, 2012–2015	0.15–0.60[a]
Asch et al., 2010	Army	Quarterly by state, 2000–2008	0.57–0.63
Simon and Warner, 2007	Army	Quarterly by state, 1996–2005	0.47 (+), 0.62 (−)[b]
Warner and Simon, 2004	Army	Quarterly by state, 1989–2003	0.53
Simon and Warner, 2003	Army	Monthly by state, 1989–1997	0.41
Warner, Simon, and Payne, 2001 (mean[c])	Various	Various, pre-drawdown	0.76

SOURCE: Adapted from Warner, 2010.
[a] Estimate varies with number of recruiters and whether and how much missions change as recruiters change.
[b] + = positive elasticity (e.g., increases in recruiters are associated with an increase in high-quality enlistments); − = negative elasticity estimate.
[c] From Appendix B of Warner, Simon, and Payne, 2001.

Recruiters do not passively process applicants; they make decisions about the level and allocation of their effort. Early estimates of recruiter productivity found that high-quality enlistments required about three times more effort than low-quality ones (Polich, Dertouzos, and Press, 1986). If recruiters faced insufficient incentives or rewards for pursuing high-quality recruits, they could substitute low-quality recruits for high-quality ones to reach their recruiting goals. As the saying goes among recruiters, "Make mission, go fish'in." An important implication is that managing recruiter effort is critical to ensuring the effectiveness of bonuses, advertising, and other recruiting programs; the Army will not experience the full market expansion effect on enlistments if recruiters cut effort when enlistments become easier to get.

Recruiters are typically managed through the Army's missioning of key categories of recruits that include high school seniors and graduates scoring in the top half of the AFQT distribution as well as the total number of Regular Army and Army Reserve contracts. Research shows that enlistments increase with higher missions, and Army recruiter productivity increases when recruiters face higher missions. For example, Knapp et al. (2018) show that the recruiter elasticity is higher when the mission-per-recruiter increases as the number of recruiters increase. But the effect of higher missions on recruiter productivity is diminishing as the difficulty of meeting the mission increases. That is, the responsiveness of recruiter productivity is lower when the mission becomes too difficult to achieve (Dertouzos and Garber, 2006).

Individual Versus Station Missioning

Over time, the Army has tried different units of management for setting missions and specifically individual-recruiter missioning versus station-level missioning. Which is more effective? Station missioning has the advantage of encouraging teamwork and cooperation among recruiters. Furthermore, it allows recruiters to take advantage of specialization if some recruiters are better at face-to-face interactions, for example, while others are better at processing paperwork. However, station missioning could undermine recruiter productivity if some team members tend to shirk their responsibilities, especially if the team is large enough to make peer monitoring more difficult.

The staggered transition from individual to station missioning in FY 2000 provided researchers with an opportunity to examine this issue. Dertouzos and Garber (2008) found that the approach that dominated in producing high-quality contracts depended on mission difficulty. When the mission was easy (low mission per recruiter) or very difficult, the individual approach dominated, but for middle levels of difficulty, station missioning dominated. Over the 1999–2001 data period considered in the 2008 Dertouzos and Garber study, station missioning increased production by about 8 percent overall relative to individual missioning, suggesting that, during this period, recruiting was achievable but not too easy. But significant changes in the mission, enlistment propensity, or economic conditions relative to the 1991–2001 period could make an individual missioning approach more effort-enhancing than a station-level approach.

Thus, it makes sense to adopt a flexible approach that requires individual achievement when the unit makes mission and also allows individual recruiters to succeed even when the station fails.

Market Quality

Missions are the most important factors explaining recruiter productivity. Beyond missions, however, the other factors that explain variations in the number of high-quality enlistment contracts signed, ranked in decreasing order of importance, are (1) the quality of the market in which the recruiter operates, (2) nationwide differences in the recruiting environment over time, (3) measured personal attributes of the recruiter, (4) station size, and (5) region of country (Dertouzos and Garber, 2006). Local market quality is the set of factors that capture the difficulty of making mission. These factors include local economic conditions, market demographics, and the size and age distribution of the veteran population. In particular, it takes less effort to sign high-quality youth (in decreasing order of importance)

- in areas with lower civilian wages
- where the available population that is qualified for military service per recruiter is high
- in markets that are urban and with populations that have relatively high proportions of non-Catholic Christians, relatively low proportions of African Americans, and children living in poverty
- in June through September (with the exception of August) compared with May
- in areas with a relatively high proportion of veterans aged less than 43 and a relatively low proportion of veterans ages 56 to 65
- in regions other than the Mountain region, except the Northeast.

Local markets differ tremendously in terms of these characteristics, and the significant differences in recruiting potential that exist among markets affect the likelihood of achieving mission. The effect of these differences could be lessened through more careful consideration by the Army of market quality factors in this list when setting recruiting missions.

Recruiter Selection Characteristics and Assignment

Recruiter productivity is also affected by recruiter selection characteristics and where they are assigned. Young recruiters (under the age of 30) are much more productive than older recruiters, as are recruiters from traditional military occupations such as combat arms and intelligence relative to recruiters in occupations with skills more readily transferred to civilian occupations, such as maintenance or logistics. These findings point to one potential problem with the private contract or civilian recruiters; these recruiters are likely to be older, retired military personnel, and therefore less effective with young prospects. In terms of assignment, recruiters who are similar to the population in their stations' territories are more successful, perhaps because potential enlistees are more likely to identify with recruiters with similar characteristics. For example, women recruiters sign more women than do men, and African American recruiters are up to 4 percent more productive than non-Hispanic white recruiters in signing high-quality prospects in markets with large black populations. Recruiters assigned to their home states are

3.3 percent more productive than similar recruiters who are not assigned to their home state, again suggesting that having things in common with the local population makes a difference for recruiter productivity.

Recruiter Incentives

Recruiters are motivated to be productive by pride in their service and their contribution to their team, as well as by different forms of recognition. Interviews with recruiters, however, suggest that recruiting is believed to be a "career killer." Research indicates that this belief is not backed up by the evidence. Analysis of the career of recruiters versus other Army personnel indicates that, on average, becoming a recruiter *increases* (not decreases) the likelihood of promotion to E6 and E7, and recruiters are more likely to stay in the Army, even after leaving recruiting. Furthermore, recruiters who perform well are promoted faster. Recruiters performing better than the station average have shorter promotion times. In short, Army career prospects are better for recruiters who perform well. An implication is that the Army should better communicate to potential recruiters how recruiting affects their career to dispel misconceptions.

The Army has also historically used an incentive plan to enhance and direct recruiter effort. Monetary incentives are not allowed by law, but recruiters who produce more enlistments overall and enlistments in specific categories could accumulate points based on their production that could lead to awards and recognition such as badges, rings, and stars. Army recruiters could also receive "mission box" points, whereby individual recruiters could earn points if their team, such as the station, met its mission for the month in specific categories such as the number of high-quality contracts.

Research shows that these incentive systems affect recruiter productivity in terms of the quality, number, and timing of enlistments (Arkes and Cunha, 2015; Asch, 1990; Asch and Heaton, 2010; Asch and Karoly, 1993). Recruiters are incentivized to increase effort when these plans are designed properly, but the plans can have perverse unintended effects if not designed well. For example, Asch and Heaton (2010) found that Army recruit screening was poorer at the end of the recruiting month, when recruiters are under pressure to meet quotas and accumulate monthly incentive plan points. They found a 10-percent higher incidence of obesity, a 30-percent increase in lower fitness ratings, and 40-percent increase in waivers among recruits who signed an enlistment contract at the end of the recruiting month relative to those signing earlier in the month. Asch and Karoly (1993) found evidence to indicate that Army guidance counselors reduced effort—evidence of "free riding"—when the Army moved to a team-based incentive plan. Dertouzos and Garber (2008) found evidence that the point system in the Army's incentive plan insufficiently rewarded high-quality enlistments; such enlistments resulted in only two-times more points, but recruiting high-quality contracts was three times more difficult for recruiters.

The results of this research suggest that it is difficult to design an effective incentive plan. Perhaps this is the reason why the Army redesigned its recruiter recognition program in FY 2011 to no longer provide points, traditional Gold Badge, Recruiter Ring, or the Glen E. Morell Rings or Medallions based on production. Instead, the Army turned to a system that gave recognition— the Master Recruiting Badge—based on tactical and technical proficiency. In FY 2017, the Army reinstated the Gold Recruiter Badge. In FY 2018, U.S. Army Recruiting Command (USAREC) approved team-based incentives—the Commanding General's Heavy Hitter award and USAREC Gold Standard—to reward the achievement of stations and companies.

By eliminating the point-and-award incentive plan that rewards production, however, the Army has turned away from a potentially powerful tool for managing recruiter productivity. The powerful effect of incentive plans (independent of missions) was documented in an older study of Army guidance counselors (Asch and Karoly, 1993). A key responsibility of guidance counselors is to channel applicants into the Army's priority occupations. During the period under study, guidance counselors were under an incentive plan that offered counselors additional points for selling a high-priority occupation. The study found that simply offering five more incentive plan points for selling a particular occupation was more than twice as effective as offering an enlistment bonus to a recruit (Figure 7). That is, it was more effective to give the seller (the guidance counselor) an incentive to sell the occupation than to give the buyer (the recruit) an incentive to "buy" the occupation. Furthermore, the budget outlay is dramatically lower; the cost of enlistment bonuses is substantial, while the cost of guidance counselor points is minimal. The study also found that the magnitude of skill-channeling effect of bonuses, discussed earlier, depends crucially on the incentives of the guidance counselors. Controlling for counselor effort, the estimated skill-channeling effect of bonuses was only 10 percent, not 45 percent, a full two-thirds lower.

Figure 7. Percentage Change in Enlistment Rate in Army Priority Occupations: Enlistment Incentives Versus Guidance Counselor Incentive Points

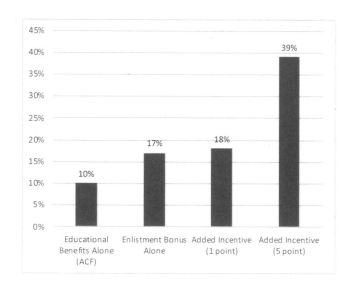

SOURCE: Asch and Karoly, 1993.
NOTE: ACF = Army College Fund.

The Army eliminated its traditional recruiter incentive awards program when Army recruiting was going relatively well in FY 2011. But the recruiting mission is now increasing, and the Army must achieve the higher mission in a tough recruiting market. The civilian unemployment rate is hitting historical lows, and budgets are tight for recruiting resources. In this environment, the Army must consider ways to improve recruiter productivity. While the FY 2018 plan changes (the Gold Standard and the Heavy Hitter award) are a step in that direction, they do not reward individual performance. A redesigned incentive plan, integrated with team-based awards, might be part of the answer. The question is whether it is possible to design an effective plan for Army recruiting personnel with minimal unintended consequences. Past lessons, together with insights from the academic literature, could help in this regard, although additional analysis is needed.

Resource Management Tools

Army recruiting is a complex and costly process. First, there are multiple objectives. These include maximizing high-quality contracts, maximizing the volume of total contracts, filling critical specialties, enhancing diversity, minimizing cost, and meeting long-term manpower goals—such as future retention of recruits and the quality of the match between the Army and the recruit—that are affected by recruiting. Second, the external environment from which recruits are drawn, such as the job market and the internal environment, including changing mission levels and deployment expectations, is ever-shifting. Finally, the Army must make resource decisions about the level and allocation of the bonus budget, advertising, and recruiters.

Complicating the decision process is the fact that the planning horizon differs for different resources; some resources can be deployed more rapidly than others, so recruiting problems on the horizon must be anticipated to ensure the right resources are in place. Furthermore, the Army has policy levers outside the traditional resources to increase supply to meet its recruiting objectives. It can grant waivers, increase the number of prior service recruits, or increase the number of non–Tier 1 or AFQT Categories IIIB recruits, as long as the Army meets the guidelines of the Office of the Secretary of Defense for overall recruit quality. But changing recruit selection criteria could create downstream attrition, occupational matching, retention, or behavioral problems.

RAND Arroyo Center recently developed a suite of integrated and sophisticated capabilities to assist the Army with its resource-level allocation problem within this complex environment. These tools are the (1) Recruiting Difficulty Index (RDI); (2) Recruit Selection Tool (RST); and (3) RRM, which incorporates both RDI and RST; but each provides insights about recruiting by itself. Together, the tools provide the Army with a capability to develop the optimal resourcing strategy to support its current and future recruiting requirements given a changing recruiting environment and alternative recruit-eligibility policies. These sophisticated tools can guide policy in a way that past research has been unable to do. In many ways, these tools are the culmination of many years of research during the all-volunteer force era about the factors affecting recruiting summarized earlier. These tools represent a major improvement in analytic capability for understanding and guiding recruiting policy because they are comprehensive and can account for the complex interactions between the social, economic, and policy environment in which the Army operates. Consequently, they can enhance confidence that recruiting resources are effectively allocated.

We briefly describe these capabilities here. The next section will discuss emerging recruiting issues and will show how these tools could be used or further extended to address some of these issues.

Recruiting Difficulty Index

The RDI is a forecast of recruiting conditions for 12- and 24-month horizons (Wenger et al., 2019a). It is intended to be a metric that anticipates changes in recruiting difficulty and the need for greater recruiting resources. The tool is especially useful for considering policy because deploying recruiting resources takes time, and the amount of time needed differs across resources. By having a forecast of what is coming down the road, policymakers can more efficiently plan and budget for different recruiting resource types. The RDI tool is based on a model that accounts for the interactions between multiple metrics of recruiting difficulty and multiple policy responses to those recruiting difficulties, including bonuses, the number of production recruiters, and use of waivers. The model also includes a set of other variables that capture economic conditions, hostile death and injury rates, and geopolitical risk. Importantly, the model predicted recruiting difficulties in 2017 and 2018, accounting for both the environment (e.g., recruiting mission, deployments, state of the economy) as well as the Army's policy responses to those changes (e.g., changes in bonuses and recruiters on duty). Because the RDI can be used with the RRM (described later), the Army has a capability to assess resource trade-offs given forecasts of recruiting difficulty.

Recruit Selection Tool

One approach to meeting recruiting challenges is for the Army to loosen selection restrictions that apply to new recruits. But what is the optimal way to do that without hurting attrition, increasing cost, or producing behavioral or other personnel problems down the road? The RST is a capability developed by RAND Arroyo Center to estimate the prospective outcomes and costs for different combination of recruits' cognitive, noncognitive, demographic, physical, and behavioral attributes (Orvis et al., 2018). These outcomes include the Delayed Entry Program (DEP), boot camp, and occupational training attrition, as well as attrition later in the first term and incidence of adverse personnel actions that include bar to reenlistment and demotion. An important aspect of the tool is that it considers the joint or combined effect, not just the isolated effects, of changing a set of attributes. By including outcomes and cost, the tool allows practitioners to consider the trade-offs between changing the characteristics of the recruit cohort—and meeting mission—and the downstream outcomes and cost of doing so.

Recruiting Resource Model

The RRM is a tool that enables Army recruiting policymakers to identify the level and mix of recruiting resources that efficiently meets the Army's recruiting objectives. It incorporates the varying recruiting environment, recruiting difficulty as measured by the RDI, cost, and the ability to change policies with respect to recruit eligibility characteristics, as provided by the RST (Knapp et al., 2018). The RRM is built around three submodels. The first focuses on the factors related to station-level Reserve Army and Army Reserve contract production, including economic conditions, recruiting difficulty, missions, recruiting resources (bonuses, recruiters, and advertising), and the size of the youth population. The second focuses on DEP attrition, capturing the probability that a contract cancellation occurs before the recruit is scheduled to access. The third focuses on cost and computes the resource cost of contracts that access in a given recruiting month. Finally, the RRM includes an optimization routine that finds the cost-minimizing level and mix of recruiting resources, given the recruiting environment and the Army's recruit eligibility policies. The RRM is highly versatile and allows the user to vary the recruiting environment, resource strategy, recruit eligibility policies, and accession goals. Consequently, it is a powerful tool to enable the Army to consider the potential cost and resource requirements for a variety of recruiting scenarios that it could face.

Navigating Current and Emerging Recruiting Challenges

The all-volunteer force has been uniformly acclaimed as a success in terms of providing the armed services with the quantity and quality of personnel required, despite dramatic changes in the military and the environment in which it operates. But recruiting, the foundation of the all-volunteer force, is challenging and costly, and while the Army has navigated challenges in the past, several emerging issues are concerning. The discussion here highlights some of these issues, possible solutions, and areas requiring additional investigation.

Military-Civil Divide

One emerging issue is a growing military-civilian divide. Researchers, policymakers, and journalists have observed and documented a low level of personal contact between the American public and the military, a low level of engagement between the two groups, and a generally shallow knowledge of what military service entails. For example, JAMRS (2016) found that less than half of surveyed American youth reported that the military has "people like them," and the proportion stating that the military would allow them to earn money for college, prepare them for a future career, have an attractive lifestyle, or be in contact with family and friends decreased markedly between 2004 and 2016. For example, the percentage reporting that joining the military would allow them to earn money for college fell from 85 percent in May 2004 to 60 percent in February 2016. This drop is even more surprising, given the introduction of the Post-9/11 GI Bill in 2009 that significantly expanded education benefits for military personnel.

Furthermore, in the 2015 survey, 65 percent of youth said that someone getting out of the military is likely or very likely to have psychological or emotional problems. The U.S. Department of Veterans Affairs indicates that the actual figure is lower than what young people perceive; only 11 to 20 percent of veterans who served in Operations Iraqi Freedom and Enduring Freedom exhibit the symptoms of posttraumatic stress disorder (U.S. Department of Veterans Affairs, 2016). A quantitative content analysis of news publications on Twitter found that the three most prevalent frames in tweets about veterans were "charity" (highlighting instances in which veterans received assistance from charitable organizations), "hero," and "victim" (highlighting mistreatment of veterans by the military and/or society, mental health issues, politics, and the Gulf War) (Parrott et al., 2018). Together, the results suggest a narrow representation of what it means to be a veteran.

A number of explanations have been put forth to explain the divide. These include the end of the draft in 1973 and of the Cold War in 1991, both of which resulted in a smaller military and a waning presence of the military in people's lives, a higher prevalence of family-connected enlistments (discussed earlier), fewer veterans among members of Congress, regional concentration of military bases, and increased differences in the characteristics and attitudes of the military and civilian society (Liebert and Golby, 2017; Morgan, 2001; Szayna et al., 2007).

Another explanation is a broader decline in civic engagement among young people in general. In a survey of the literature, Flanagan and Levine (2010) document that young adults are less likely than their 1970s counterparts to exhibit nine of out ten important characteristics of citizenship, such as voting. The exception is volunteering. Analysis of survey data of high-school seniors indicates that few seniors express trust in the government or elected officials but that youth who planned to graduate from a four-year college were more civically inclined than their peers with two-year degrees or no college plans (Syversten et al., 2011). Flanagan and Levine also argue that some but not all of the decline could be due to a more-protracted developmental period because of delays in marriage, family formation, and stable jobs. Civic engagement increases with age as roles and connections become more stable. But it appears that younger generations are not catching up with their elders even as they move through their 20s.

JAMRS (2016) analyzed data from a nationally representative survey of high-school seniors and found that, in some respects, high-school seniors today have similar life values and work values to high school seniors in the 1970s but very different values in other respects. Like youth from earlier periods, today's youth continue to emphasize the importance of family, careers, and personal relationships, but they are more likely to want socially impactful careers that also allow them to experience life outside work.

While these trends have broader societal implications, from the standpoint of successful recruiting, the Army needs to develop a proactive, practical, and cost-effective strategy for bridging the divide that is informed by metrics, data, and analysis. The Army needs to evaluate which outreach efforts should be considered, to whom they should be directed (e.g., which segment of the youth market, which influencers), what key information should be communicated, and how success could and should be measured. It is critical to have evidence about the return on investment of recruiting efforts that are intended to positively affect youth and influencer attitudes because the lack of evidence has led to elimination by Congress of such efforts, as was the case of military sponsorship of sporting events such as NASCAR.

Societal Trends Limiting Recruit Eligibility and Supply

As noted earlier, less than 30 percent of young adults are estimated to meet enlistment eligibility criteria, thereby limiting the supply of eligible youth. Furthermore, broader societal trends with respect to changing attitudes toward marijuana use, mental health, and the use of psychotropic drugs could further restrict enlistment eligibility. Other societal trends, such as rising college attendance, affect the supply of recruits willing to enlist. One part of a strategy for bridging the military-civilian divide that could also address these recruit-eligibility and supply issues is to reconsider, adapt, and possibly loosen recruit selection criteria to more closely reflect societal trends, especially in the young adult population. The key is to do so without degrading military performance. Examples of areas in which this has been done in the past are the loosening of the Army's tattoo policy and the Army's addition of recruit strength testing to body mass index metrics to address rising obesity rates among American youth.

Research shows that more young people are experiencing major depressive episodes and using antidepressants. Antidepressant use within the past 12 months is an enlistment disqualifier. For example, analysis of data from the National Surveys on Drug Use and Health for 2005 to 2014 indicates that the 12-month prevalence of major depressive episodes increased over this period, from 8.7 percent to 11.3 percent among adolescents (ages 12–17) and from 8.8 percent to 9.6 percent among young adults (ages 18–25), with the increase greater among young women than young men (Mojtabai, Olfson, and Han, 2016).

The Army does not want to enlist those who will not respond well to the stresses of military service or combat or who might even pose an insider threat. But it is also possible that the current enlistment qualification standards are too stringent even for those with active diagnoses of behavioral health issues; the standards may lack adequate nuances, thereby inadvertently screening out people who suffer from milder forms of depression or less-debilitating issues who might still perform well in the military setting. The Army should determine the extent to which current mental health standards disqualify otherwise high-quality enlistees and make use of the RST, described earlier, to assess the trade-offs in terms of the cost and performance outcomes of changing these standards.

Societal attitudes toward marijuana use are also changing, as indicated by the recent legalization of marijuana in a number of states. While marijuana use is still unlawful at the federal level, the change raises questions about whether past marijuana use degrades military performance and whether the Army should revisit its enlistment standards with respect to marijuana use as a means of expanding enlistment supply. The Army should assess civilian trends in marijuana use among its key recruiting market segments, decomposed by states where marijuana use is legal. It should examine the extent to which current standards disqualify otherwise high-quality enlistees and assess whether enlistees with reported marijuana use perform differently than enlistees with similar characteristics who do not report use. The RST, together with RRM, should also be used to measure the trade-offs of relaxing the marijuana use standard. Without additional analysis, it is unclear the extent to which changing waiver policy with respect to mental health or marijuana use could affect readiness or cost, but it is interesting to note that even a doubling in the percentage of accessions receiving waivers for nontraffic legal offenses—another category of waiver that is one of the largest waiver categories— from 10 to 20 percent was predicted by RST to produce almost no change in first-term attrition rates and an overall cost savings to the Army because expanding waivers would reduce recruiting costs (Orvis et al., 2018, Appendix B).

Another societal trend is the rising percentage of high-school graduates who immediately transition to college following high-school graduation. From 2000 to 2015, the immediate college enrollment rate increased from 63.3 percent to 69.2 percent (National Center for Education Statistics, undated), although the percentage varied during this period. The percentage is higher for females than males, but, in both cases, the percentage increased over this period. Given that military recruiters focus their recruiting efforts on U.S. high schools, the high rate of college attendance puts military service immediately following high school in direct competition with college attendance. To expand enlisted supply to the Army, it is key to make college attendance complementary rather than a substitute for military service. The Post-9/11 GI Bill and the tuition-assistance program provide military personnel with resources to attend college, enabling college attendance and making military service complementary, but these programs are typically used during or, in the case of the GI Bill, after active duty service is completed.

Another approach the Army could take is to recruit college students nearing graduation or to target college dropouts. Research from the early 2000s indicated that the two-year market—two-year students and two-year dropouts—has the greatest enlistment potential in terms of having characteristics associated with eligibility to enlist and interest in enlistment (Asch and Kilburn, 2003). Further analysis of the characteristics of two-year dropouts indicated that their likelihood of dropping out was related to the high cost of college, inability to get financial aid, not being listed as their parents' dependents, and working while in school. These characteristics suggest that dropping out of two-year programs is associated with affordability of college, an area that the Army and the other services could address through such programs as the Post-9/11 GI Bill and tuition assistance. In addition, the characteristics that predicted dropping out were not largely related to characteristics that made them ineligible to enlist. Research also indicates that Army recruits with postsecondary education perform better in terms of lower DEP loss, basic training loss, and fewer adverse personnel flags, such as rank reduction and bar to reenlistment (Orvis et al., 2018). Furthermore, those who separate are less likely to do so because of performance and conduct issues, drug abuse, or serious offenses. In short, the research points to the strong potential of targeting recruiting toward the enlistment of the two-year college market, especially dropouts.

Related to the rising percentage of high-school graduates attending college is the rise in college debt. According to the National Center for Education Statistics, about half of all undergraduates take out loans, with total borrowing per full-time equivalent undergraduate student increasing by 56 percent between academic years 2000–2001 and 2010–2011 (Wei and Horn, 2013). Repaying this debt has become increasingly difficult, especially for those who do not complete a degree, and relief from college debt could be especially attractive to this group. This argues for the value and possible expansion of the Army's Loan Repayment Program for eligible recruits.

Targeting the enlistment of older recruits is another possible approach to expanding supply. Older recruits are more likely to have postsecondary education, but research indicates that even when controlling for their better education, better aptitude scores, and other characteristics, older recruits perform better in terms of retention and promotion (Rostker, Klerman, and Cotugno, 2014). An advantage of targeting older individuals is that they initially chose not to join the military when they graduated from high school; instead, they made the decision to join at a later time. They tried other career or educational paths and wanted another option. Consequently, older individuals could be more highly propensed to join the military than their younger counterparts. The percentage of Army accessions who are older is significant and increasing but still only makes up about one-third of all accessions. Specifically, the percentage that is age 21 or older was 35 percent in 2016, up from 31 percent in 2000 (Office of the Under Secretary of Defense for Personnel and Readiness, 1997–2016). The tools developed by RAND Arroyo Center, such as RRM and RST, could be used to further investigate the effect and cost-effectiveness of targeting the enlistment of older recruits and the two-year college market.

A final societal trend relevant to the Army is the decline in the number of hours worked by young men—a decrease of 12 percent between 2000 and 2015 for men ages 21 to 30 (Aguiar et al., 2017). One explanation for this decline in labor-market hours by a key segment of the Army's target marget is a decline in the demand by employers for their labor over this period. But Aguiar et al. (2017) found evidence to suggest that a key explanation is that the marginal value of leisure increased over this period for this group as a result of improvements in the technology of recreational computer use and video gaming. The study found that over an eight-year period, beginning in the mid-2000s, young men increased their recreational computer use and video gaming by nearly 50 percent, and this increase occurred to some extent at the expense of working hours.

The greater demand for leisure by young men as a result of increased gaming suggests the Army might target its recruiting message to a greater extent in a way that highlights opportunities in the Army for those interested in video games and recreational computer use. It also points to the importance of effective targeting of youth via the internet and social media in addition to traditional media such as television. The Army's social media presence on such platforms as GoArmy.com and its Twitter and Facebook accounts provide a basis for doing so, but recent research suggests areas of possible improvement, such as creating content more tailored to audience interest and developing additional metrics to measure communication effectiveness (Wegner et al., 2019b).

Gaps in Recruiting Management

These emerging issues, as well as the geographic concentration of recruits from the Southeast, raise the question of whether the Army requires additional approaches to managing recruiting. In particular, they raise the question of whether the Army could more successfully disaggregate and target its outreach, recruiting message, and resources to improve recruiting effectiveness.

The Army's recruiting message has evolved over time, from "be all you can be" to "an Army of one" to "Army strong" to the current focus on the "Army team." A successful slogan is one that clearly and memorably communicates the Army story and inspires public support and young people to enlist. But the Army's outreach with respect to its resourcing decisions and advertising content could be too one size fits all. Targeting could be important if young people struggle to see how an Army career fits in with their interests—interests that, along with other opportunities, vary across groups.

Individuals in different market segments have different perceptions about military service. They have different reasons for joining the military and different external opportunities. Older segments of the youth population (ages 22–24 rather than 17–21) have a more heightened perception of the risks of serving in the military, and older recruits are more likely to state that job security, developing leadership skills, and providing for a family are reasons to join the military (JAMRS, 2017b). Individuals in the southern United States have a higher propensity to enlist than the national average and are more likely to join for intangible benefits such as patriotism (JAMRS, 2018). In New England and parts of the Midwest, where the economic context is stronger and educational attainment is higher, people are more likely to state reasons related to their career aspirations as reasons to join (JAMRS, 2018). Geographic differences in enlistment propensity and eligibility might also change over time as a result of economic booms and busts in different regions, such as the coal mining boom and bust. For example, research shows that high school graduation rates, as well as college enrollment, fell in West Virginia, North Dakota, and Montana as a result of the shale boom in those states, suggesting that eligibility and propensity may change over time even within a region (Rickman, Wang, and Winters, 2017).

The Army needs to investigate if and how it can improve its recruiting outreach and resource effectiveness through better targeting to different market segments. Research has been limited in this area, but available analysis suggests that resource effectiveness could differ with market segment. For example, Asch, Heaton, and Savych (2009) estimated Army enlistment supply models by race and ethnicity and found that black Army high-quality enlistments increased more with recruiters than they did with enlistment bonuses, relative military pay, and educational benefits, while Hispanic Army high-quality enlistments are highly responsive to changes in military pay and Army educational benefits but less responsive to bonuses. No research is available on the effectiveness of targeted outreach and advertising content or of bonus and recruiter effectiveness in different regions. For example, outreach efforts in New England might focus on the educational and career opportunities the Army affords, while those in the South might focus on intangible benefits. No doubt recruiters in these areas already do this informally, but those efforts are not strategically supported at the national level with targeted advertising content or other coordinated outreach efforts.

Tools should be used and enhanced as needed to permit assessment of more-refined targeting strategies. For example, the RRM could be used or enhanced to incorporate enlistment models for specific segments, such as college-market recruits, older recruits, and recruiting outcomes in different regions. An enhanced RRM would permit an assessment of the cost-effectiveness of more targeting, and the trade-offs of more targeting versus a more nationally oriented policy.

The Army's current branding focuses on teamwork, and that focus is also reflected in the team-based incentive program for Army recruiters. Team-based incentives have advantages such as encouraging cooperation among recruiters and allowing for specialization of tasks in larger stations. But individual incentives could be effective if they are well-structured. The Army should consider a combination approach that rewards both team and individual performance. Given that early research suggests that incentives for recruiters (or, specifically, guidance counselors) can be as or more effective than monetary incentives targeted toward recruits, a well-structured incentive plan for recruiters could be highly cost-effective. The RRM could be extended to incorporate recruiter incentives and a capability to assess the trade-offs of incentivizing recruiters versus recruits.

Finally, Army recruiting decisions should be fully integrated with retention resource decisionmaking. On the one hand, it might be more cost-effective to increase reenlistment bonuses and special pays to retain personnel rather than to increase resources to recruit and train more personnel when strength requirements change, especially in occupations with high training costs such as cryptologic linguists. On the other hand, increased retention increases personnel costs because of higher retention bonus, incentive costs, compensation, and retirement accrual costs associated with a more experienced force. Analysis is required of the trade-off between the cost retaining versus recruiting and training personnel to meet a given strength target.

Conclusion

This report highlights research findings that can help the Army navigate current and emerging recruiting challenges. It also highlights a number of promising areas for further investigation. Given the recruiting challenges the Army currently faces, research in areas that will assist the Army in expanding enlistments should be the focus. Among the options discussed in this report, the following are likely to be promising in terms of efficacy of expanding enlistment supply:

- The Army should take advantage of recently developed tools, such as the RRM, RST, and RDI, to identify the level and mix of resources needed to meet its current and emerging challenges (informed by estimates of recruiting difficulty provided by the RDI), and identify the optimal way to change recruit selection criteria. These tools should be refined to enable the Army to also consider resource allocation, including mission allocation, across-market segments, and the optimal targeting of resources across geographic areas and among segments such as older individuals and the college dropout market.
- The Army should also study feasible ways to expand recruit eligibility, especially on characteristics that are changing in the general population, such as marijuana use and the use of antidepressants.
- Research shows that recruiter management and recruiter incentive programs in particular, matter in terms of influencing recruiter productivity. The Army's current team incentive program should be expanded to integrate individual recruiter incentives, but additional research is required to identify the best ways to do that.

Finally, recruiting resourcing decisions should be made in coordination with retention resource decisions. The Army requires a modeling capability to identify the return on investment to recruiting versus retaining an additional high-quality soldier and the cost-experience trade-off of increasing retention instead of accessions.

Abbreviations

AFQT	Armed Forces Qualification Test
DEP	Delayed Entry Program
DoD	U.S. Department of Defense
FY	fiscal year
RDI	Recruiting Difficulty Index
RMC	regular military compensation
RRM	Recruiting Resource Model
RST	Recruit Selection Tool
USAREC	U.S. Army Recruiting Command

(This page is intentionally left blank.)

References

Aguiar, Mark, Mark Bils, Kerwin Kofi Charles, and Erik Hurst, *Leisure Luxuries and the Labor Market Supply of Young Men*, Cambridge, Mass.: National Bureau of Economic Research, Working Paper 23552, June 2017. As of March 20, 2019:
https://www.nber.org/papers/w23552.pdf

Arkes, Jeremy, and Jesse M. Cunha, "Workplace Goals and Output Quality: Evidence from Time-Constrained Recruiting Goals in the U.S. Navy," *Defence and Peace Economics*, Vol. 26, No. 5, 2015, pp. 491–515.

Asch, Beth J., "Do Incentives Matter? The Case of Navy Recruiters," *Industrial and Labor Relations Review*, Vol. 43, No. 3, February 1990, pp. 89-S–106-S.

Asch, Beth J., and Paul Heaton, *An Analysis of the Incidence of Recruiter Irregularities*, Santa Monica, Calif.: RAND Corporation, TR-827-OSD, 2010. As of October 4, 2018:
https://www.rand.org/pubs/technical_reports/TR827.html

Asch, Beth J., Paul Heaton, James Hosek, Paco Martorell, Curtis Simon, and John T. Warner, *Cash Incentives and Military Enlistment, Attrition, and Reenlistment*, Santa Monica, Calif.: RAND Corporation, MG-950-OSD, 2010. As of October 2, 2018:
https://www.rand.org/pubs/monographs/MG950.html

Asch, Beth J., Paul Heaton, and Bogdan Savych, *Recruiting Minorities: What Explains Recent Trends in the Army and Navy?* Santa Monica, Calif.: RAND Corporation, MG-861-OSD, 2009. As of October 4, 2018:
https://www.rand.org/pubs/monographs/MG861.html

Asch, Beth J., and Lynn A. Karoly, *The Role of the Job Counselor in the Military Enlistment Process*, Santa Monica, Calif.: RAND Corporation, MR-315-P&R, 1993. As of October 4, 2018:
https://www.rand.org/pubs/monograph_reports/MR315.html

Asch, Beth J., and M. Rebecca Kilburn, "The Enlistment of Potential College Students," in M. Rebecca Kilburn and Beth J. Asch, eds., *Recruiting Youth in the College Market: Current Practices and Future Policy Options*, Santa Monica, Calif.: RAND Corporation, MR-1093-OSD, 2003:
https://www.rand.org/pubs/monograph_reports/MR1093.html

Asch, Beth J., John A. Romley, and Mark E. Totten, *The Quality of Personnel in the Enlisted Ranks*, Santa Monica, Calif.: RAND Corporation, MG-324-OSD, 2005. As of October 2,

2018:
https://www.rand.org/pubs/monographs/MG324.html

Asch, Beth J., and John T. Warner, "Should the Military Retirement System Be Reformed?" in J. Eric Fredland, Curtis Gilroy, Roger D. Little, and W. S. Sellman, eds., *Professionals on the Front Line: Two Decades of the All-Volunteer Force*, Washington, D.C.: Brassey's, 1996.

Buddin, Richard, *Success of First-Term Soldiers: The Effects of Recruiting Practices and Recruit Characteristics*, Santa Monica, Calif.: RAND Corporation, MG-262-A, 2005. As of October 2, 2018:
https://www.rand.org/pubs/monographs/MG262.html

Christensen, Garret S., "Occupational Fatalities and the Labor Supply: Evidence from the Wars in Iraq and Afghanistan," *Journal of Economic Behavior and Organization*, Vol. 139, No. C, July 2017, pp. 182–195.

Dertouzos, James N., and Steven Garber, *Is Military Advertising Effective? An Estimation Methodology and Applications to Recruiting in the 1980s and 90s*, Santa Monica, Calif.: RAND Corporation, MR-1591-A, 2003. As of October 4, 2018:
https://www.rand.org/pubs/monograph_reports/MR1591.html

Dertouzos, James N., and Steven Garber, *Human Resource Management and Army Recruiting: Analyses of Policy Options*, Santa Monica, Calif.: RAND Corporation, MG-433-A, 2006. As of October 4, 2018:
https://www.rand.org/pubs/monographs/MG433.html

Dertouzos, James N., and Steven Garber, *Performance Evaluation and Army Recruiting*, Santa Monica, Calif.: RAND Corporation, MG-562-A, 2008. As of October 4, 2018:
https://www.rand.org/pubs/monographs/MG562.html

Flanagan, Constance, and Peter Levine, "Civic Engagement and the Transition to Adulthood," *Future Child*, Vol. 20, No. 1, Spring 2010, pp. 159–179.

Ford, M., B. Griepentrog, K. Helland, and S. Marsh, *The Strength and Viability of the Military Propensity-Enlistment Relationship: Evidence from 1995–2003*, Washington, D.C.: Joint Advertising and Marketing Research Studies, Office of the Undersecretary of Defense for Personnel and Readiness, U.S. Department of Defense, JAMRS Report No. 2009-005, April 2009, not available to the general public.

Hosek, James, Beth J. Asch, Michael G. Mattock, and Troy D. Smith, *Military and Civilian Pay Levels, Trends, and Recruit Quality*, Santa Monica, Calif.: RAND Corporation, RR-2396-OSD, 2018. As of February 1, 2019:
https://www.rand.org/pubs/research_reports/RR2396.html

Joint Advertising and Marketing Research Studies, *Generational Values and Their Impact on Military Recruiting*, Washington, D.C.: Office of the Undersecretary of Defense for Personnel and Readiness, U.S. Department of Defense, October, 2016, not available to the general public.

JAMRS—*See* Joint Advertising and Marketing Research Studies.

Joint Advertising and Marketing Research Studies, *Family History of Military Service*, Washington, D.C.: Office of the Undersecretary of Defense for Personnel and Readiness, U.S. Department of Defense, July 2017a, not available to the general public.

Joint Advertising and Marketing Research Studies, *Overview of the Older Recruiting Market: Insight on the New Recruits Ages 22–24*, Washington, D.C.: Office of the Undersecretary of Defense for Personnel and Readiness, U.S. Department of Defense, May 2017b, not available to the general public.

Joint Advertising and Marketing Research Studies, *Summer 2017 Propensity Update: Youth Poll Study Findings*, Washington, D.C.: Office of the Undersecretary of Defense for Personnel and Readiness, U.S. Department of Defense, February 2018, not available to the general public.

Kane, Tim, *Who Bears the Burden? Demographic Characteristics of U.S. Military Recruits Before and After 9/11*, Washington, D.C.: Center for Data Analysis, the Heritage Foundation, CDA05-08, November 7, 2005. As of October 4, 2018:
https://www.heritage.org/defense/report/who-bears-the-burden-demographic-characteristics-us-military-recruits-and-after-911

Kilburn, M. Rebecca, and Jacob Alex Klerman, *Enlistement Decisions in the 1990s: Evidence from Individual-Level Data*, Santa Monica, Calif.: RAND Corporation, MR-944-OSD/A, 1999. As of October 4, 2018:
https://www.rand.org/pubs/monograph_reports/MR944.html

Kleykamp, Meredith A., "College, Jobs, or the Military? Enlistment During a Time of War," *Social Science Quarterly*, Vol. 87, No. 2, June 2006, pp. 272–290.

Knapp, David, Bruce R. Orvis, Christopher E. Maerzluft, and Tiffany Tsai, *Resources Required to Meet the U.S. Army's Enlisted Recruiting Requirements Under Alternative Recruiting Goals, Conditions, and Eligibility Policies*, Santa Monica, Calif.: RAND Corporation, RR-2364-A, 2018. As of October 2, 2018:
https://www.rand.org/pubs/research_reports/RR2364.html

Lewin Group, Inc., *Qualified Military Available (QMA): Final Technical Report*, Falls Church, Va.: Lewin Group, Inc., October 10, 2013.

Liebert, Hugh, and James Golby, "Midlife Crisis? The All-Volunteer Force at 40," *Armed Forces and Society*, Vol. 43, No. 1, January 2017, pp. 115–138.

Lien, Diana S., Kletus Lawler, and Robert Shuford, *An Investigation of FY10 and FY11 Enlisted Accessions' Socioeconomic Characteristics*, Alexandria, Va.: Center for Naval Analyses, DRM-2012-U-001362-1REV, November 2012. As of October 4, 2018: https://www.cna.org/CNA_files/PDF/DRM-2012-U-001362-1Rev.pdf

Mojtabai, Ramin, Mark Olfson, and Beth Han, "National Trends in the Prevalence and Treatment of Depression in Adolescents and Young Adults," *Pediatrics*, Vol. 138, No. 6, December 2016.

Morgan, Matthew J., "Army Recruiting and the Civil-Military Gap," *Parameters*, Vol. 31, No. 2, Spring 2001, pp. 101–107.

National Center for Education Statistics, "Fast Facts: Immediate Transition to College," webpage, undated. As of October 9, 2018: https://nces.ed.gov/fastfacts/display.asp?id=51

Office of the Under Secretary of Defense, Personnel and Readiness, *Population Representation in the Military Services*, webpage links to reports from 1997 to 2016, Washington, D.C.: U.S. Department of Defense, 2017. As of October 5, 2018: https://www.cna.org/research/pop-rep

Orvis, Bruce R., Christopher E. Maerzluft, Sung-Bou Kim, Michael G. Shanley, and Heather Krull, *Prospective Outcome Assessment for Alternative Recruit Selection Policies*, Santa Monica, Calif.: RAND Corporation, RR-2267-A, 2018. As of October 2, 2018: https://www.rand.org/pubs/research_reports/RR2267.html

Parrott, Scott, David L. Albright, Caitlin Dyche, and Haley Grace Steele, "Hero, Charity Case, and Victim: How U.S. News Media Frame Military Veterans on Twitter," *Armed Forces and Society*, Vol. 44, No. 3, July 2018, pp. 1–21.

Pew Research Center, *The Military-Civilian Gap: Fewer Family Connections*, Washington, D.C.: Pew Research Center, November 23, 2011. As of October 4, 2018: http://www.pewsocialtrends.org/2011/11/23/the-military-civilian-gap-fewer-family-connections/

Polich, J. Michael, James N. Dertouzos, and James S. Press, *The Enlistment Bonus Experiment*, Santa Monica, Calif.: RAND Corporation, R-3353-FMP, 1986. As of October 4, 2018: https://www.rand.org/pubs/reports/R3353.html

Rickman, Dan, Hongbo Wang, and John Winters, "Is Shale Development Drilling Holes in the Human Capital Pipeline?" *Energy Economics*, Vol. 62, February 2017, pp. 283–290.

Rostker, Bernard D., Jacob Alex Klerman, and Megan Zander Cotugno, *Recruiting Older Youths: Insights from a New Survey of Army Recruits*, Santa Monica, Calif.: RAND Corporation, RR-247-OSD, 2014. As of October 4, 2018:
https://www.rand.org/pubs/research_reports/RR247.html

Simon, Curtis J., Sebastian Negrusa, and John T. Warner, "Educational Benefits and Military Service: An Analysis of Enlistment, Reenlistment, and Veterans' Benefit Usage 1991–2005," *Economic Inquiry*, Vol. 48, No. 4, October 2010, pp. 1008–1031.

Simon, Curtis J., and John T. Warner, "Cash Today or College Tomorrow? Incentives and Intertemporal Choice in the Army and Navy," unpublished manuscript, Clemson, S.C., Clemson University, 2003.

Simon, Curtis J., and John T. Warner, "Managing the All-Volunteer Force in a Time of War," *Economics of Peace and Security Journal*, Vol. 2, No. 1, 2007, pp. 20–29.

Simon, Curtis J., and John T. Warner, "The Supply Price of Commitment: Evidence from the Air Force Enlistment Bonus Program," *Defence and Peace Economics*, Vol. 20, No. 4, August 2009, pp. 269–286.

Statista, "Unemployment Rate in the United States from 1990 to 2018, by Age," webpage, 2019. As of July 18, 2019:
https://www.statista.com/statistics/217882/us-unemployment-rate-by-age/

Syversten, Amy K., Laura Wray-Lake, Constance A. Flanagan, D. Wayne Osgood, and Laine Briddell, "Thirty-Year Trends in U.S. Adolescents' Civic Engagement: A Story of Changing Participation and Educational Differences," *Journal of Research on Adolescence*, Vol. 21, No. 3, September 2011, pp. 586–594.

Szayna, Thomas S., Kevin F. McCarthy, Jerry M. Sollinger, Linda J. Demaine, Jefferson P. Marquis, and Brett Steele, *The Civil-Military Gap in the United States: Does It Exist, Why, and Does It Matter?* Santa Monica, Calif.: RAND Corporation, MG-379-A, 2007. As of October 4, 2018:
https://www.rand.org/pubs/monographs/MG379.html

U.S. Department of Labor, Bureau of Labor Statistics, "Graphics for Economic News Releases," webpage, July 2019. As of August 23, 2019:
https://www.bls.gov/charts/employment-situation/civilian-unemployment-rate.htm

U.S. Department of Veterans Affairs, "How Common Is PTSD?" webpage, September 24, 2018. As of October 5, 2018:
https://www.ptsd.va.gov/understand/common/index.asp

Warner, John T., "The Influence of Economic Factors on Military Recruiting and Retention: Evidence from Past Studies," unpublished manuscript, Falls Church, Va., The Lewin Group, October 2010.

Warner, John T., and Curtis J. Simon, "Updated Estimates of U.S. Military Enlistment Supply," unpublished manuscript, Clemson, S.C.: Clemson University, October, 2004.

Warner, John T., Curtis J. Simon, and Deborah M. Payne, *Enlistement Supply in the 1990's: A Study of the Navy College Fund and Other Enlistment Incentive Programs*, Arlington, Va.: Defense Manpower Data Center, DMDC Report No. 2000-015, April 2001. As of October 8, 2018:
http://www.dtic.mil/dtic/tr/fulltext/u2/a390845.pdf

Watkins, Shanea J., and James Sherk, *Who Serves in the U.S. Military? Demographic Characteristics of Enlisted Troops and Officers*, Washington, D.C.: Center for Data Analysis, Heritage Foundation, CDA08-05, August 21, 2008. As of October 4, 2018:
https://www.heritage.org/defense/report/who-serves-the-us-military-the-demographics-enlisted-troops-and-officers

Wei, Christina Chang, and Laura Horn, *Federal Student Loan Debt Burden of Noncompleters*, Washington, D.C.: U.S. Department of Education, NCES 2013-155, April 2013. As of March 25, 2019:
https://nces.ed.gov/pubs2013/2013155.pdf

Wenger, Jeffrey B., David Knapp, Parag Mahajan, Bruce R. Orvis, and Tiffany Tsai, *Developing a National Recruiting Difficulty Index*, Santa Monica, Calif.: RAND Corporation, RR-2637-A, 2019a. As of July 12, 2019:
https://www.rand.org/pubs/research_reports/RR2637.html

Wenger, Jennie W., Heather Krull, Elizabeth Bodine-Baron, Eric Larson, Joshua Mendelsohn, Tepring Piquado, and Christine Anne Vaughn, *Social Media and the Army: Implications for Outreach and Recruiting,* Santa Monica, Calif.: RAND Corporation, RR-2686-A, 2019b. As of July 12, 2019:
https://www.rand.org/pubs/research_reports/RR2686.html

Wenger, Jennie W., and Cathleen M. McHugh, *Is Recruiting More Difficult in "Blue" States? Evidence from Past Election Years*, Alexandria, Va.: Center for Naval Analyses, CRM D0017556.A2/Final, 2008.

Wenger, Jennie W., Trey Miller, Matthew D. Baird, Peter Buryk, Lindsay Daugherty, Marlon Graf, Simon Hollands, Salar Jahedi, and Douglas Yeung, *Are Current Military Education Benefits Efficient and Effective for the Services?* Santa Monica, Calif.: RAND Corporation, RR-1766-OSD, 2017. As of October 4, 2018:
https://www.rand.org/pubs/research_reports/RR1766.html